"I wonder what that flower is ?"

Lady Bird Johnson has stimulated us to enjoy the free growing wildflowers we take for granted. So Richards Lyon, after recording on film many of these Napa roadside beauties, enlisted the aid of Jake Ruygt, student of our wildflowers, to create this photo story. Once we can recognize what "*is there*", it is always a surprise and joy to see how much more we "*see*". Hopefully, that little patch of color that just went by, in the past unrecognized, will now through familiarity add to the excitement of an afternoon's drive through our Valleys. Because their blossoms add so much to the palette of roadside beauty, we have taken the liberty of placing a number of our native shrubs among the wildflowers.

CALIFORNIA POPPY *Eschscholzia californica*
Family Poppy

This plant is one of the most recognizable of California native plants. Its golden orange flowers are robust in spring when they seem to radiate sunlight. This perennial produces smaller and paler flowers as the spring passes, progressing toward yellow in summer. The California Poppy is identified by a rim (torus) apparent below the attachment of the petals. Poppies prefer open sunny places on rocky soils.

Find Highway 12, Pope Valley, most roadsides
Blooms February - September

FRYING PAN POPPY *Eschscholzia caespitosa*
Family Poppy

This poppy, commonly known as The Frying Pan Poppy, is smaller than its relative, the California Poppy. It does not have the rim (torus) below the petals. It appears about a month later on sunny steep slopes and can be easily missed as one drives by. This annual flower produces seeds that can lie dormant in the soil for many years and can sprout by the thousands after a brush fire.

Find Chiles & Pope Valley Rd., Highway 128, Redwood Road
Blooms March - May

WILD RADISH   *Raphanus sativus*
Family   Mustard

This plant closely resembles the very common field mustard. In fact it sometimes has yellow flowers but they are pale. The flowers typically range from white to purple with the whole range of colors found in large populations. The plant was introduced to this area from Europe. The green radish is a variety of the same species.

Find   Silverado Trail
Blooms   February - July

MILKMAIDS   *Cardamine californicus*
Family   Mustard

Milkmaids are the native counterpart to field mustard which was probably introduced to this state by Spanish missionaries. Its white flowers can sometimes be found as early as December or January in warm winters, making it the first wildflower of the year. Four distinct varieties occur in Napa County. The flowers in some are pink and the leaves of some are red underneath. They can be found in wooded and brushy areas or infrequently in open grassland.

Find   Sage Canyon Road,   Monticello Road
Blooms   February - May

COMMON MANZANITA
Arctostaphylos manzanita
Family   Heather

This is the most widely adapted of the eight varieties of manzanita found in Napa County. It usually grows as an understory in woodlands and forest. But often it is a common member of chaparral covered slopes. It can range from four to over fifteen feet in height. The flowers are like delicate white urns, pendant in a many flowered cluster. The word "manzanita" comes from the early Spanish settlers and means "little apple", so named because of the small red fruit.

Find   Monticello Road, Atlas Peak Road
Blooms   January - April

BUCK BRUSH   *Ceanothus cuneatus*
Family   Buckthorn

This shrub and its several close relatives make up a part of the chaparral community, prominent on the east side of the Napa Valley. This particular species is usually white flowered but occasionally has pale blue flowers. The musty fragrance of plants in bloom can be overpowering on a warm spring day.

Find   Dry Creek Road, Howell Mountain Road
Blooms   March - May

STRIPED WHITE EYES

Nemophila menziesii var. atomaria
Family   Waterleaf

This is the white flowered variety of Baby Blue Eyes. Its delicate flowers are about the size of a nickel. It can be found in open grassy meadows, in woodlands, and among chaparral. This native plant is low-growing and is usually found in good numbers.

Find   Soda Canyon Road, Pope Valley
Blooms   March - May

FOOTHILL NEMOPHILA

Nemophila heterophylla
Family   Waterleaf

This delicate annual is not known for showy displays but its dainty white flowers are commonplace in our woodlands. The leaves of this plant are curious in form with spatula-shaped divisions. Nemophila means "woodland loving", referring to the habitat of this species and several other relatives that can be found on oak covered slopes.

Find   Snell Valley Road, Chiles & Pope Valley Rd.
Blooms   March - June

COMMON PHACELIA *Phacelia distans*
Family   Waterleaf

Phacelia (pronounced fa-seal-ia) is an annual that has an affection for rocks. It is most often seen among rock outcrops
or among loose cobbles on slopes. Its dull cream flowers are
not eye-catchers unless captured in numbers following a spring
rain. Then they glisten in the sun.

Find   Soda Canyon Road
Blooms   March - June

IMBRICATE PHACELIA   *Phacelia imbricata*
Family   Waterleaf

This native perennial is not usually found in great numbers,
but if you search around rocky outcrops you can expect to
find it. It occurs in many areas of the county. Its creamy white
flowers emerge from a tight coil of buds that continue to open
as the stems uncoil.

Find   Monticello Road, Chiles & Pope Valley Road
Blooms   March - June

YERBA SANTA *Eriodictyon californicum*
Family   Waterleaf

This plant acquired its name from early Spanish settlers who considered it a "blessed herb". It was used by the Spanish, and Native Americans before them, to make a tea to cure colds and asthma. This shrub is usually found in colonies because it spreads by its running rootstock. The leaves usually develop a sticky-sooty appearance. The flowers are white in this county, while they are lavender in the Sierra Nevada Mountains.

Find   Atlas Peak Road, Pope Canyon Road
Blooms   April - July

CHAMISE *Adenostoma fasciculatum*
Family   Rose

This is the most common shrub to be found in Napa County. In fact the Spanish used to refer to the chaparral community, which this native plant dominates as "chamisal". It looks rather dismal during the long summer but is covered with small white blossoms in late spring. It is well adapted to this climate and quickly sprouts after a wildfire.

Find   Atlas Peak Road,   Soda Canyon Road
Blooms   May - June

WESTERN MORNING-GLORY
Calystegia occidentalis
Family   Morning-glory

Like most morning-glorys, this plant clambers over other plants or trails along the ground. It does not occur in large numbers. The plants are usually found scattered here and there. The flowers of this native are quite showy, sometimes dangling from a branch of a roadside shrub.

Find   Hwy.128, Monticello Dam, Oakville Grade
Blooms   April - July

FIELD BINDWEED   *Convolvulus arvensis*
Family   Morning-glory

Bindweed is a member of a family of plants that twist and wind themselves up whatever vegetation surrounds them. This plant was introduced from Eurasia and has become a trouble-some weed to all who live with it. The white flowers can be seen through much of the year and they become particularly noticable in vineyards and cultivated fields.

Find   Silverado Trail, St. Helena Highway
Blooms   April - October

MINER'S LETTUCE   *Claytonia perfoliata*
Family   Purslane

This plant is easily identified by the circular leaf surrounding the stem. A number of varieties of this plant can be found in our area with different leaf shapes and colors. The leaves of this plant have been used as greens and eaten raw. The plant prefers some shade and therefore is most often found in oak woodlands.

Find   Monticello Road,   Redwood Road
Blooms   February - June

CALIFORNIA MANROOT   *Marah fabaceus*
Family   Gourd

This perennial herb twists itself around trees and shrubs to capture the light it needs. It can sometimes be found climbing on fences as if someone planted it there. The small cream flowers are crisp and simple in form but appear as a small sprays of stars.

Find   Redwood Road,   Monticello Road
Blooms   February - May

BELLARDIA *Bellardia trixago*
Family   Snapdragon

This annual was introduced to this country from the Mediterranean region. It resembles our native owl's clover in growth
habit, size, and habitat. For this reason it is often seen in our
grasslands near its native counterparts. Its showy arrange-
ment of pink and white flowers make it an attractive "weed",
often prominent in pastures.

Find   Napa Valley, Carneros Valley
Blooms   April - June

VALLEY TASSELS *Castilleja attenuata*
Family   Snapdragon

The slender stems of this native plant make it inconspicuous
until the flowers begin to emerge. The flowers are rather
small and it is the modified leaves (bracts) that give the flower
heads most of their color. These heads which form on the tip
of the stem appear like tassels. The plant likes grassy areas
on flats or gradual slopes, particularly when the soil is shallow and rocky.

Find   Pope Valley, Carneros Valley
Blooms   March - May

WOODLAND STAR   *Lithophragma affine*
Family   Saxifrage

This attractively sculptured flower is not very abundent but seems to show up in many places. The flowers are openly arranged along a long slender stem that is easily taken by the wind. This species is differentiated from its look-alike relative (hillside star) by the tapered point of attachment of the flower to the stem. The flowers are white in each case.

Find   Chiles & Pope Valley Road
Blooms   March - May

WHITEWHORL LUPINE
Lupinus microcarpus var. densiflorus
Family   Pea

This lupine is not very common in Napa County but is a prominent feature of a spring trip through Pope Valley. It forms a carpet of flowers along the road that leads into Pope Canyon. The flowers are white but on closer inspection a flush of pink can be seen.

Find   Pope Canyon Road
Blooms   April - June

QUEEN ANNE'S LACE   *Daucus carota*
Family   Carrot

This clustered flower seems to be everywhere on the side of the road, whether in California or Turkey, always lighting up an otherwise dull barren soil Its head of flowers may be up to a foot in diameter, and it seems to weather all seasons.

Find   Highways 29 and 121
Blooms   All year round

COMMON MEADOW FOAM
Limnanthes douglasii
Family   False Mermaid

This annual is aptly named for it appears in flower like a creamy foam in wet fields. It prefers areas that flood periodically, so this plant can sometimes be seen in great numbers where and when puddles dry up in the spring. Some particularly noteworthy populations can be over-seen from the lower part of Oat Hill Mine Road trail. A chemical has been extracted from one meadow-foam that is proving important as a substitute for sperm whale oil.

Find   Calistoga, Silverado Trail
Blooms   February - May

HAYFIELD TARWEED
Hemizonia congesta ssp. luzulifolia
Family   Sunflower

This plant was given its name because it grows rapidly after the farmer's hay has been cut and bailed. It blooms all summer long and continues until cool weather settles in. There are three varieties in our area that are identified by white or yellow flowers and whether or not the stems are sticky from top to bottom. This one is the most common. Its pungent odor can be detected by rolling down the window while driving in the American and Jameson Canyons on a warm summer evening.

Find   Napa-Vallejo Highway
Blooms   April - September

COMMON YARROW   *Achillea millefolium*
Family   Sunflower

This common perennial has confused botanists for some time. It was decided recently that this same species occurs throughout the world, one of the very few flowering plants to do so. Its showier relatives with pink or yellow flowers are used in floral arrangements. Look closely at the flowers to discover that the apparent flower is actually comprised of many small flowers in a "composite" head.

Find   Silverado Trail
Blooms   March - June

WHITE HYACINTH *Triteleia hyacinthina*
Family   Amaryllis

Native Hyacinth and Brodiaea bulbs were an important part
of the diet of Native Americans. Although the bulbs are very
small, these plants were sometimes so numerous that collect-
ing them was a worthwhile endeaver. It is said that digging
the bulbs in the proper fashion stimulate quick replacement.
The white hyacinth prefers broad open grasslands and is one
that has managed to survive the plow in some areas..

Find   Pope Valley
Blooms   April - May

FREMONT'S STAR LILY *Zigadenus fremontii*
Family   Lily

This Star Lily is the most common of three species occurring
in Napa County. The two foot tall stem topped with numerous cream colored flowers is most conspicuous on bushy roadsides, sprouting forth in small openings. The plant grows
from a small bulb as do other lilies. After forest fires it may
appear in greater numbers.

Find   Deer Park Road
Blooms   February - May

BOWL-TUBED IRIS *Iris macrosiphon*
Family   Iris

This is one of the three native irises to be found in Napa
County, and is by far the most common. The beautifully
sculpted flowers of this plant vary greatly in color from one
individual to the next. They are most commonly violet but
some areas contain yellow or white flowered plants. This
plant is usually found in partial shade of trees or shrubs in
porous soils.

Find   Monticello Road, Chiles & Pope Valley Road
Blooms   April - June

GIANT TRILLIUM *Trillium chloropetalum*
Family   Lily

This curious plant produces only three leaves on its stems
each year and only a single flower. This is one of the most
regal of our flowering plants. It is not conspicuous because it
seems to hide in the forest shade, often in the midst of poison
oak. Its stems are about one foot tall and the flowers are
white or a deep rose-purple.

Find   Redwood Road, Spring Mountain Road
Blooms   February - May

CALIFORNIA BUTTERCUP
Ranunculus californicus
Family   Buttercup

The flowers of this wiry-stemmed perennial plant are glossy due to a wax on the petals. The brilliant sulfury color of the flowers brighten many meadows and woodlands in Napa County. Its close relative, the Western Buttercup, resembles this plant but can be differentiated by flowers that always have five petals.

Find   Highway 29, Silverado Trail
Blooms   February - June

COMMON FIDDLENECK   *Amsinckia menziesii*
Family   Borage, Forget-Me-Not

Fiddleneck is an adaptable native annual that inhabits pastures and cultivated fields. Its persistence in hayfields trouble farmers for the plant is toxic to livestock. Plants vary greatly in size from six inch unbranched plants to a robust three feet. The tiny trumpet-shaped flowers open as the flower stalk elongates and uncoils. The yellow flowered form shown in the photo is less common than the orange flowered form which also has larger flowers.

Find   Silverado Trail, Highway 128
Blooms   March - June

PACIFIC STONECROP   *Sedum spathulifolium*
Family   Stonecrop

As the name suggests, this plant can be found on rock out-crops. It often grasps onto vertical walls with apparently no soil. This plant can be identified by its rounded leaves about one inch long. The flowers are borne on a short stalk and open into a tight cluster.

Find   Chiles & Pope Canyon Road, Monticello Rd.
Blooms   May - June

DWARF STONECUP *Parvisedum pumilum*
Family   Stonecup

This plant is one of a group of native succulents that inhabit rocky areas. Dwarf Stonecup can be found on thin gravelly soils that collect on flat rock outcrops. It can sometimes be found in great numbers but usually is confined to small patches.

Find   Atlas Peak Road
Blooms   March - May

JOHNNY JUMP-UP *Viola pedunculata*
Family   Violet

This charming plant is not easily spotted because it lies low to the ground. It is one of the earlier flowers to light up the grassland in spring. Its bright yellow flowers are backed with purple.The purple veins in the throat act as a landing beacon for pollinating insects. The plants form little tufts in pastures and sometimes in fence rows.

Find   Highway 12 near Sonoma County line
                   Coombsville Road, Fourth Avenue
Blooms   February - April.

SUN CUP *Camissonia ovata*
Family   Evening Primrose

The habitat of this plant is similar to that of the garden dandelion. It likes moist grassy places. The leaves all originate from the base of the plant and the flowers are yellow. The difference is that this species is not a sunflower as is the dandelion. It has four petals and the apparent stem of the flower is actually a long flower tube with the seeds forming near ground level.

Find   Soda Canyon Road
Blooms   March - May

KLAMATH WEED   *Hypericum perforatum*
Family   St. John's Wort

Introduced from Europe this species became so common in our pastures that a method of control needed to be found. To date the most successful biological control project, the introduction of a beetle, has aided greatly in reducing the plant to a managable level. Its golden yellow flowers are numerous on a branched stalk about two feet tall.

Find   Highway 29 north
Blooms   May - September

FOOTHILL LOMATIUM   *Lomatium utriculatum*
Family   Carrot

This low growing perennial can be quite common in grassland and woodland plant communities. Its leaves resemble that of a carrot. The roots are somewhat swollen although they are usually divided. The yellow flowers are borne on stoutish stems that seldom exceed six inches in height. The plant is sometimes called Wild Parsnip because of its odor.

Find   Chiles & Pope Valley Rd., Snell Valley Rd.
Blooms   February - May

SEEP-SPRING MONKEYFLOWER
Mimulus guttatus
Family   Snapdragon

This engaging plant is quite variable in the size of flowers and stems. Mature individuals can be found that are a few inches high. Others may be two feet tall. The flowers of this species show a number of maroon spots that may serve as markings for insect pollination. This yellow flower can be found in numbers along rocky seasonal watercourses and seepy banks on slopes. Thus its name speaks for itself.

Find   Wild Horse Valley Road
Blooms   March - September

STICKEY MONKEYFLOWER
Mimulus aurantiacus
Family   Snapdragon

This shrub is a common member of our chaparral communities. Its drought tolerance permits it to bloom over a long period. The flowers are usually orange but occasionally the color will pale towards white. In recent years horticultural varieties have become available.

Find   Silverado Trail, Monticello Road
Blooms   March - August

BUTTER AND EGGS *Triphysaria eriantha*
Family   Snapdragon

This plant is one of three similar species that are found in our grasslands. This one can easily be identified by its red stems and purplish tooth-like "galea" on the flower. This annual plant can sometimes form blankets in pastures and on shallow soils on gradual slopes, usually open and sunny.

Find   Carneros, Pope Valley
Blooms   March - May

SMOOTH OWL'S CLOVER *Triphysaria versicolor var. faucibarbata*
Family   Snapdragon

This plant resembles butter-and-eggs except that it lacks red in the galea and stems. It also prefers deeper clay soil. Its lemon-yellow flowers form carpets in fields south of Napa in mid-spring and in good years form a sea of yellow in PopeValley. The plant is not really a clover although its compact head of flowers resembles that of some clovers.

Find   Hwy. 29 south, Pope Valley
Blooms   March - June

MOTH MULLEIN *Verbascum blattaria*
Family   Snapdragon

These plants are easy to identify by their tall slender stalks lined with yellow flowers. Three kinds of mulleins have made their way into the wilds of Napa County, having taken origin in Eurasia. They can usually be found on roadsides or other areas where the ground has been barren.

Find   Silverado Trail
Blooms   May - October

DOUGLAS' WALLFLOWER *Erysimum capitatum*
Family   Mustard

This uncommon spring wildflower is a prominent feature of rock walls and rocky slopes. It is an eye-catcher with its brilliant flowers. The stems of this plant can reach three to four feet in height. A close relative grows on the Antioch dunes and has been featured on postage stamps due to its endangered status.

Find   Monticello Road
Blooms   April - June

BULL CLOVER *Trifolium fucatum*
Family   Pea

Clovers belong to a genus which literally means "three leaves". This refers to the leaves which are divided into three leaflets. Bull Clover is a robust native clover with flowers that swell up as the fruits begin to mature. The flowers are a pale lemon yellow when first opening but soon become pinkish or reddish. This plant prefers deep soils and open grassland. It is common on serpentine soils which are toxic to many plants.

Find   Pope Valley, Snell Valley
Blooms   April - June

CALIFORNIA FALSE LUPINE
Thermopsis macrophylla
Family   Pea

While appearing very similar to other lupines, this plant can be separated from them by the presence of two leaf-like bracts at the base of each leaf stem. This plant spreads by underground rhizomes leading to dense stands of bright yellow flowers. This species shows up in grassy openings of forests or occasionally in open grassland or woodland.

Find   Atlas Peak Road, Steel Canyon Road
Blooms   April - June

NARROW-LEAFED MULE EARS

Wyethia augustifolia
Family   Sunflower

The flowers of this plant resemble that of other Mule Ears found in Napa Valley, but this plant has narrow leaves. It resembles California Helianthella but its leaves are symmetrical at the base and the plant does not appear woody. This species prefers the open sun of meadows or flats, particularly where the ground remains wet after winter rains.

Find   Chiles & Pope Valley Road
Blooms   April - July

MULE EARS   *Wyethia glabra*
Family   Sunflower

The broad sometimes shiney leaves of this plant make it easy to identify. The three to four inch wide flowers of the plant make it the largest of our native sunflowers. Each plant produces a few too many flowers which look like a natural bouquet. Similar plants of the same genus are common at higher elevations in the Sierra Nevada. This species is found in grassy opening in woodlands and forests.

Find   Monticello Road, Chiles & Pope Valley Road
Blooms   March - May

CALIFORNIA HELIANTHELLA

Helianthella californica

Family   Sunflower

This perennial is slightly woody at the base, distinguishing it from a few look-a-like sunflowers. Its daisy-like flowers stand out among the brush where they prefer to find protection. The flower stems are up to two feet high with a cluster of strap-shaped leaves at the base.

Find   Howell Mountain Road
Blooms   April - May

WOOLLY SUNFLOWER *Eriophyllum lanatum*

Family   Sunflower

Single yellow flowers are usually suspended on long bare stems, although on serpentine soil very compact plants are found. Most striking is the fine loose cobwebby hair covering the stems and leaves. They prefer sunny places such as rocky roadbanks.

Find   Dry Creek Road, Howell Mountain Road
Blooms   May - August

SMOOTH LAYIA *Layia chrysanthemoides*
Family   Sunflower

The Layia is closely related to the better known "Tidy Tip". The flowers of this species sometimes put on a brilliant display in open grasslands. They often grow in the presence of owl cover, valley tassels, and goldfields. This is one of several grassland species that are becoming more difficult to find as our grasslands disappear.

Find   Pope Valley, Old Highway 29 south of Napa
Blooms   March - July

CALIFORNIA GOLDFIELD
Lasthenia californica
Family   Sunflower

This bright little annual often carpets grassy slopes or flats where the soil is rocky or shallow. It is aptly named for it can turn a field golden with its daisy-like flowers that are about one-half inch in diameter. As common as these plants are, they are fast disappearing in the face of development as ranches are replaced by vineyards and houses.

Find   Pope Valley, Atlas Peak Road
Blooms   March - May

CALIFORNIA CUDWEED
Gnaphalium californicum
Family   Sunflower

This biennial herb can be up to three feet tall with several stems from the base of the plant. These plants are usually found alone or with a few companions in forest openings. The leaves are a yellowish-green or grayish when young. The flowers are made conspicuous by the pearly silver bracts called phyllaries, These surround the minute yellowish flowers.

Find   Silverado Trail
Blooms   March - August

YELLOW STAR THISTLE   *Centaurea solstitialis*
Family   Sunflower

This rapacious plant fills many fields and roadsides in this county. It may have been introduced here from the Mediterranean region by early Spanish ranchers. It has become the bane of modern ranchers and hikers. The bright yellow flowers are surrounded by several straw colored thorns that easily pierce one's clothing.

Find   Silverado Trail, Highway 29
Blooms   May - October

BLOW WIVES   *Achyrachaena mollis*
Family   Sunflower

The flower of this annual wildflower appears as if it is not fully opened (note bottom right corner). It is the broad shiny "awns" of the fruit that catch the eye. They somewhat resemble the fruit of the dandelion but are not fluffy. They thus do not carry for long distances in the wind. The plant likes open flat areas in grasslands.

Find   Pope Valley, Napa Valley
Blooms   April - May

BRISTLEY OX-TONGUE   *Picris echioides*
Family   Sunflower

This sometimes stout annual made its way here from England where it reportedly inhabits the famous white cliffs of Dover. It has become well established here as a weed in gardens and pastures. It has curious swellings at the base of the hairs on its leaves.

Find   Highway 29
Blooms   June - December

ANNUAL MOUNTAIN DANDELION
Agoseris heterophylla
Family   Sunflower

The flowers of this annual resemble the common dandelion which was introduced from Europe for salad greens. The native dandelion usually has few yellow flowers but can be quite showey when found in colonies. This plant prefers open grassy areas with rocky soils and gradual slopes. The feathery fruits are carried far in the wind.

Find   Pope Canyon Road, Wooden Valley Road
Blooms   April - June

MICROSERIS   *Microseris douglasii*
Family   Sunflower

The fruit of this plant appear much like a garden dandelion. This much more delicate forb (flowering annual) is a native relative of the wayfarer. Its flowers remain closed unless adequate light is available and do not make their presence known until the fruit is mature. The flattened bristles of the fruit carry the seeds into the wind.

Find   Pope Valley
Blooms   April - May

GOLDEN FAIRY LANTERN
Calochortus amabilis
Family   Lily

This plant is a member of a genus of very photogenic native lilies. They carry such colorful names as star tulip, mariposa lily, gold nuggets, and fairy lantern. In most of the species the bowl of the flower faces upward, but in this and several others the bowl faces downward and hangs like a lantern from narrow stems. The plant has been adopted by Angwin as the town flower. It is a favorite of many.

Find   Howell Mountain Road
Blooms   April - June

GOLD NUGGETS   *Calochortus luteus*
Family   Lily

These beautiful native flowers might be considered analogous to the tulips of Asia Minor. It is produced by a bulb that is buried several inches into the soil and gives rise to a stem topped by a few exquisite golden yellow flowers. They are easily overlooked in the dry grasses of late spring but not difficult to find if you take the time to look. They prefer open grassy flats and gradual slopes.

Find   Monticello Road, Howell Mountain Road
Blooms   April - June

MISSION BELLS   *Fritillaria affinis*
Family   Lily

The fritillaries are a group of plants that received great interest horticulturally, for some species produce large showy flowers. Most of our natives produce neither large nor showy flowers but always create interest because of the unusual pattern of colors they exhibit. These plants are not normally found in great numbers but can be expected in forests where there is some dappled light.

Find   Redwood Road, Mt. Veeder Road
Blooms   February - May

FRENCH BROOM   *Genista monspessulana*
Family   Pea

This evergreen shrub may be recognized by some as a horticultural plant. It is one of those species that was brought to this country from the Mediterranean region with the best of intentions to add to our palette of garden plants, but it has become an invader of our natural landscape. This plant may be seen along many of our roadsides where it is slowly marching into the forest or woodland. Its bright yellow flowers produce a bumper crop of seeds.

Find   Dry Creek Road, Howell Mountain Road
Blooms   March - May

GRAND HOUNDS TONGUE
Cynoglossum grande
Family   Forget-Me-Not

This stout perennial is one of the first flowers to bloom in spring, showing up on wooded or bushy slopes in partial shade. It appears in a natural bouquet with a cluster of rich blue flowers on stems that reach above a cluster of broad leaves at the base of the plant. The flowers produce a fruit with a rough surface resembling that of a dog's tongue.

Find   Monticello Road, Chiles & Pope Valley Road
Blooms   March - May

ROYAL LARKSPUR   *Delphinium variegatum*
Family   Buttercup

This plant is one of four or five blue flowered larkspurs that can be found in Napa County. What appears to be spreading petals on this plant are actually sepals. These enclose the petals of a flower in bud. The petals of this plant are pale violet or whitish. The flowers are usually few in number but they are showey. They can be found on gradual slopes where there are grassy openings in woodland or chaparral communities.

Find   Atlas Peak Road, Howell Mountain Road
Blooms   April - May

FALSE BABY STARS *Linanthus androsaceus*
Family   Phlox

This small annual usually grows in crowded clusters, making for an attractive display of lavender or blue blossoms. The flowers are borne at the tops of the plants and are few to numerous on the four to six inch tall plants. Look for the plant on roadbanks or slopes with grassy openings. They like places with partial shade from trees or shrubs.

Find   Dry Creek Road, Sage Canyon Road
Blooms   March - June

BABY BLUE EYES
Nemophila menziesii ssp. menziesii
Family   Waterleaf

This cheery flowered annual is readily recognized by its baby blue flowers with pale centers that are about the size of a penny. The flowers are sometimes violet tinged. They are occasionally seen in great numbers in our grasslands or moist fields. This plant seldom exceeds six inches in height so it is more likely to be found when strolling or biking along country roads.

Find   Pope Valley,   Silverado Trail
Blooms   February - May

BIRD'S EYE GILIA *Gilia tricolor ssp. tricolor*
Family   Phlox

This delicate annual is one our most exquisite natives. It can be found on gradual slopes, usually where the soil is shallow and competing grasses grow sparsely. Large stands of this plant can be seen from a distance as a soft blue sheet. Take time to observe this flower close enough to see stamens that at maturity are covered with a blue pollen.

Find   Snell Valley Road, Highway 128 east of
                Moskowite Corner
Blooms   March - May

LADY BLOOM *Ceanothus parryi*
Family   Buckthorn

This evergreen is one of the most attractive of our native shrubs. Its deep blue flowers are borne in large clusters that sometimes cover the entire plant. It can be found in brush-lands but is most often found in openings among forests. A close relative with sky blue flowers can be found on serpentine soil in Butts Canyon.

Find   Monticello Road, Howell Mountain Road
Blooms   April - May

DOUGLAS'S LUPINE *Lupinus nanus*
Family   Pea

Douglas's Lupine is one those plants that make the hillsides of California woodlands outstanding displays of wildflowers in springtime. In some years these flowers show up in such multitudes that many a grassy slope is fully carpeted in a royal blue. This is a close relative of the "Blue Bonnet" which is well known in the midwest and is the state flower of Texas. One local relative, Lupinus bicolor, that has smaller flowers may also be seen.

Find   Pope Valley,   Wooden Valley Road
Blooms   March - May

SILVER LUPINE *Lupinus albifrons*
Family   Pea

It is the elongated spikes of sweet pea-shaped flowers that make lupines distinctive from other plants. This species is the only lupine in Napa County that forms an upright shrub. It is content growing on rocky soil around rock outcrops or on roadcuts. The flowers are usually blue but vary to rose violet in some individuals.

Find   Mt. St. Helena on Highway 29
Blooms   March - June

CHICORY   *Cichorium intybus*
Family   Sunflower

The rich blue flowers of this plant stand on tall wiry stems, often filling fields. The flowers can be seen in mid-day but they disappear during the afternoon as the blossoms roll up. This plant was introduced here from Europe where it has long been used as a substitute for a flavoring agent to coffee and for its greens.

Find   Silverado Trail, many vacant lots in down-
                  town Napa
Blooms   June - October

FOOTHILL PENSTEMON
Penstemon heterophyllus
Family   Snapdragon

This wirey perennial is slightly woody at the base. It is sub-dued and inconspicuous until the grass has begun to dry in late spring. Then it bursts forth with brilliant tube-shaped flowers. These flowers begin as yellowish buds, then turn pink when first opening, and then complete their development in a luminous blue color. This plant can be found on rocky roadbanks and slopes.

Find   Monticello Road, Pope Canyon Road
Blooms   April - July

BLUE EYED GRASS   *Sisyrinchium bellum*
Family   Iris

The leaves of this plant are narrow like a grass but they emanate from the base of the plant. This member of the Iris family has flowers which are radially symmetrical, unlike the true Irises. The flowers open during the day and close at night. The "eye" of the plant is actually yellow and the lower tips are blue. Occasionally, white flowers can be found. This plant can be discovered in moist grasslands.

Find   Silverado Trail, Monticello Road
Blooms   March - May

WILD HYACINTH   *Dichelostemma capitatum*
Family   Amaryllis

This is undoubtedly the most common member of this family in Napa County. It can be found on most slopes wherever their is adequete sunlight. In some wet areas many more plants are present than are evident from the number of flowers. It is said that new bulbs may take five years before they produce flowers. The flower stems of this species vary from several inches to two feet in height and the leaves are usually beginning to wither as the flowers open.

Find   Atlas Peak Road
Blooms   March - May

HARVEST BRODIAEA *Brodiaea elegans*
Family   Amaryllis

Harvest Brodiaea (pronounced broe-dea) is a name given to a number of early summer flowering species of this genus. They are usually shielded by taller grasses but the elegant purple flowers appear as the grasses dry, thus bringing them into focus. The flowers open one at a time from a single stalk that arises from a small bulb. The plant is most apt to be found in open grassland although it also appears among brush and open woodland.

Find   Soda Canyon, First Avenue
Blooms   April - July

ITHURIEL'S SPEAR *Triteleia laxa*
Family   Amaryllis

The flowers of this plant are quite similar to those of the Harvest Brodiaea. In fact at one time they were recognized as belonging to the same genus. The flowers of this plant are more numerous and usually open one at a time. Its blue trumpet flowers are borne on one to two foot tall stalks. In some areas the growth may be heavy.

Find   Sage Canyon Road
Blooms   April - June

CHEESE WEED *Malva sylvestris*
Family   Mallow

This tough perennial has become commonplace around towns and in cultivated areas. Its attractive pink flowers are not very conspicuous but the leaves are distinctive in this rather robust plant. It can be a tough competitor of garden plants. The flowers resemble that of a Hibiscus, a popular ornamental member of the same family.

Find   Napa, St.Helena
Blooms   All year

HARTWEG'S CHECKERMALLOW
Sidalcea hartwegii
Family   Mallow

This slender stemmed annual appears when grasses dry in late spring. Its crisp pink flowers are about the size of a quarter and they dapple a grassy slope. These flowers quickly capture the attention of the wandering photographer or naturalist.

Find   Atlas Peak Road
Blooms   March - June

CUT-LEAVED GERANIUM *Geranium dissectum*
Family   Geranium

This annual plant has become ubiquitous in garden and natural landscapes. It was introduced from Europe. Its small pink flowers resemble that of many horticultural species.

Find   Silverado Trail
Blooms   March - June

REDMAIDS *Calandrinia ciliata*
Family   Purslane

This plant is one of the few natives that have adapted well to agricultural activities. Its brilliant rose-pink flowers can be found speckling the ground between vineyard rows in early spring. Its spreading branches make it inconspicuous if other vegetation grows too tall. The leaves are slightly fleshy as is characteristic of many plants in the Purslane family.

Find   Oak Knoll Avenue
Blooms   February - May

SCARLET PIMPERNEL   *Anagallis arvensis*
Family   Primrose

The name of this species is well known from English litera-
ture and it is in Europe that this plant originated. Although
the flowers are usually a scarlet-orange, a form of this plant
can be found with sapphire flowers. These are quite conspicuous in garden landscapes but are also frequent in natural plant communities such as brushy areas where there is
partial shade.

Find   Atlas Peak Road
Blooms   March - July

HENDERSON'S SHOOTING STAR
Dodecatheon hendersonii
Family   Primrose

Shooting Stars resemble the horticultural cyclamen with its
petals that are folded away from the stamens of the flower.
In fact they belong to the same family. This elegant little native is usually less than twelve inches tall with a small cluster
of pink or, rarely, white flowers. They prefer the well drained
soils found near chaparral and sometimes appear in multitudes in these areas.

Find   Soda Canyon Road,   Oakville Grade
Blooms   February - May

CALIFORNIA FUCHSIA *Zauschneria californica*
Family   Evening Primrose

This delightful shrub always provides wonder as to where it finds its resources, It emerges on rocky outcrops, often on south slopes. It grows slowly during spring and summer and doesn't begin to flower until summer is on its way out. Then it blooms rather profusely until the weather turns cold. This plant has become a popular addition to the rock gardens created in recent years.

Find   Monticello Road
Blooms   August - October

RED LARKSPUR *Delphinium nudicaule*
Family   Buttercup

The unusual shape of this plant makes it unmistakable. The brilliant red flowers seem to radiate light. Even on a cloudy day they appear bright. It can be found on roadside cut banks where it projects its flowers towards the roadway. The plant can be found in forested areas with sunny openings.

Find   Redwood Road, Dry Creek Road
Blooms   March - June

RED RIBBONS *Clarkia concinna*

Family   Evening primrose

This may qualify as the most elegant wildflower in Napa County. Its uniquely contoured petals are a bright pink and thus make this otherwise small plant very visible where it occurs in numbers. At least three kinds of Clarkia find an affection for roadcuts, making them easy targets for drive-by wildflower lovers. Red Ribbons can be found as summer approaches and the grasses have dried.

Find   Dry Creek Road
Blooms   May - July

ELEGANT CLARKIA *Clarkia unguicalata*

Family   Evening Primrose

This annual plant begins to show its color as grasses dry in late spring. It can be easily spotted if you take the time to look on steep roadbanks where it likes to grow in patches. The plants are quite lanky, often standing two feet tall, and are narrowly branched above. It is one of a number of Clarkias that find our roadsides agreeable and it is identified by its four diamond-shaped petals.

Find   Silverado Trail,   Sage Canyon Road
Blooms   May - June

SLENDER CLARKIA   *Clarkia gracilis*
Family   Evening Primrose

This annual is always an eye catcher if you happen to be driving through Chiles Valley in late spring. It congregates in large patches in grassy openings of serpentine chaparral. It is the high levels of nickel and magnesium, among other minerals, that make serpentine a haven to plants that tolerate these otherwise toxic conditions. This Clarkia seems to thrive here and is identified by the buds that remain bent downward until ready to display their brilliant colors.

Find   Chiles Valley Road, Butts Canyon Road
Blooms   April - July

WINE-CUP CLARKIA   *Clarkia purpurea*
Family   Evening Primrose

This late spring annual appears after the grasses have dried to a golden brown. It is often plentiful in forest openings, roadcuts and open flat fields. Individual flowers vary in color from a deep wine-purple to a pink with a darker center. Its buds are always erect as opposed to slender clarkia

Find   Dry Creek Road,   Howell Mountain Road
Blooms   April - July

BRIGHT BABY STARS   *Linanthus parviflorus*
Family   Phlox

This dainty annual stands three to six inches tall with flowers that tend to congregate at the tops of the plants. They can be quite showy when found in patches that often are made up of thousands of plants. The flowers are usually pink but can be white. An occasional patch may be all white. The plant prefers shallow rocky soils on gradual slopes.

Find   Highway 128 east of Moskowite Corner
Blooms   March - June

ROSE CLOVER   *Trifolium hirtum*
Family   Pea

This clover was introduced from Europe as a forage crop for livestock. As with many species brought from that region it is well suited to our Mediterranean climate and has become a common element of our grasslands and woodlands. In Napa County it is one of the over twenty varieties of clover of which one-third are immigrants. This one is identified by the red-veined swelling on the leaf that subtends the flower.

Find   Silverado Trail, Atlas Peak Road
Blooms   April - May

WHITETOP CLOVER   *Trifolium variegatum*
Family   Pea

This plant is usually found in seasonally wet areas that are grassy. In fact its presence in late spring and early summer can tell you what its like in that location in the winter and early spring. You can usually find cattle taking advantage of these nutritious areas for clover is high in protein. Plants belonging to the Pea family usually have specialized organisms on their roots that help them acquire nitrogen for growth.

Find   Pope Valley
Blooms   March - July

TOMCAT CLOVER   *Trifolium wildenovii*
Family   Pea

This is probably the most common of the native clovers of Napa County. Its pretty little flowers are arranged in a neat whorl at the end of each branch. The leaves are composed of three slender leaflets. The plant can be found on many roadbanks in mid-spring.

Find   Howell Mountain Road
Blooms   March - June

PACIFIC PEA *Lathyrus vestitus*
Family   Pea

The flowers and leaves of this plant resemble the garden sweet pea and they belong to the same genus. The native is more delicate and has several leaflets on each leaf. The flowers are attractively marked with orchid veins on pink-to-white petals. The flowers often dry a rusty color. This plant can be found scrambling over bushes or grass on the slopes of forests and woodlands. They seem to congregate in patches.

Find   Monticello Road, Partrick Road
Blooms   April - June

VALLEY LUPINE
Lupinus microcarpus var. microcarpus
Family   Pea

A variety of colorful lupines can be found in the area around Lake Berryessa. Different varieties of this species have yellow, white, or pink flowers. This particular variety is our only annual lupine with all individuals having pink flowers. It can be found along roadsides in gravelly soil. This lupine of grasslands has blue-green leaves.

Find   Highway 128
Blooms   April - June

WINTER VETCH *Vicia villosa*
Family   Pea

As with most of our Vetches, this one was introduced from
Europe as a forage crop for livestock, recalling a life in Napa
County that is fading. There are two varieties in our area,
this one having silky hairs on its stems. The plant can be
found in fields, pastures, and roadsides. It prefers full sun.

Find   Silverado Trail, Sage Canyon Road
Blooms   March - July

COMMON VETCH *Vicia sativa var nigra*
Family   Pea

This bright little sweet pea-like flower has become common
in woodland communities. It has made its way here from
Europe as a forage crop for livestock. Flowers are usually
borne singly along the nodes of the stems on this plant, these
stems are usually two feet or more in length.

Find   Silverado Trail, Soda Canyon Road
Blooms   April - June

CHINESE HOUSES *Collinsia heterophylla*
Family   Snapdragon

This beautiful annual displays the most intricate pattern of colors among the local flora. Its tiers of flowers resemble the layers of a Chinese pagoda. The plant is found in small groups and occasionally in large colonies in woodlands. It seems to prefer partial shade and grassy slopes.

Find   Snell Valley, Chiles & Pope Valley Road,
              Atlas Peak Rd.
Blooms   March - June

BLUE-EYED MARY *Collinsia sparsiflora*
Family   Snapdragon

Four different varieties of this species can be found in Napa County. They range from small flowered to rather showy flowers, and with nearly white flowers to plants with violet flowers having white and purple spots. This dainty plant is found in grassy woodlands and brushlands. Sometimes it shows up in eye-catching masses.

Find   Monticello Rd., Sage Canyon Rd., Hwy. 128
Blooms   March - May

FELT PAINTBUSH *Castilleja foliolosa*
Family   Snapdragon

The felt of this perennial herb is gray hair which provides the plant with a protection from drying out. This plant is therefore well adapted to dry rocky sites in chaparral. Its flowers normally appear red due to the red tips of the upper leaves called bracts. They can also rarely be found with individuals that have yellow bracts. A few close relatives with red flowers are equally as common as this species but are not gray-hairy.

Find   Soda Canyon Road, Dry Creek Road
Blooms   March - July

INDIAN WARRIOR *Pedicularis densiflora*
Family   Snapdragon

This plant is often confused with a fern when seen without flowers. It is an interesting plant because the leaves are often purplish in color. It is one of a group of plants in the Snapdragon family which are partially parasitic on other plants. Many of the plants in this group have petals that are joined into a beaklike tube. Indian Warrior can usually be found in forests with a mixture of trees such as oak, madrone, and fir.

Find   Monticello Road, Howell Mountain Road
Blooms   January - June

PURPLE OWL CLOVER   *Castilleja densiflora*
Family   Snapdragon

This formerly very common plant is becoming harder to find as open flat pastures disappear. This plant usually keeps the company of goldfields, smooth layia, and valley tassels. Together they make a memorable display of mid-spring wildflowers. The stems are hairless and there are few branches above. A look-alike species with hairy stems can be found on wooded or bushy slopes.

Find   Pope Valley, Henry Road
Blooms   March - May

SALSIFY , Oyster Plant   *Tragopogon porrifolius*
Family   Sunflower

This robust biennial was introduced here from southern Europe where it has been cultivated in the vegetable garden. Its stout fleshy stems with milky sap and purple flower are distinctive but the large brown ball of plum-tipped seeds set it apart from any other plants native or naturalized in Napa County. The term "Tragopogon" means "goat's beard" and refers to the characteristic seed head. It prefers roadsides and other disturbed open areas.

Find   Cuttings Wharf Road, Calistoga
Blooms   April - July

ITALIAN THISTLE *Carduus pycnocephalus*
Family   Sunflower

This thistle was introduced from Europe and has become to woodlands what Star Thistle has become to grasslands and is a major problem for livestock and recreationists. The pink flowers are attractive and efficient seed producers. This plant becomes prevelant as grasses dry in the spring and continues until the hot summer sun dries the soil. It is less abundant where livestock grazing is moderate or light.

Find   Silverado Trail
Blooms   May - July

MILK THISTLE *Silybum marianum*
Family   Sunflower

This robust annual displays a large pink flower. It was introduced from the Mediterranean region and has become a pest in overgrazed pastures. It is easily identified by its spiney leaves which are marbled with whitish veins.

Find   Silverado Trail, Fourth Avenue, Jameson
          Canyon Road
Blooms   May - July

TWINING SNAKE LILY *Dichelostemma volubile*
Family   Amaryllis

It is the twining stems of this plant that give it its name. While other species in this genus stand alone, this one climbs up the stems of shrubs and grasses. The stems may be five feet long with a small cluster of pink flowers at the tip and no leaves to be found. The plant is particularly conspicuous in the year following a fire in chaparral.

Find   Highway 128
Blooms   May - June

SHEEP SORREL *Rumex acetosella*
Family   Buckwheat

The reddish flowers of this perennial plant are no more than stamens or pistils, for petals are lacking. This plant, introduced from Europe, spreads with underground rhizomes so that one plant may form a patch of many stems. It prefers open flat grassy areas though at times it can be found in gravelly soil.

Find   Pope Valley
Blooms   March - August

Stonecrest Press
600 Stonecrest Napa, CA 94558
(707) 255 8702

ISBN 0-9616004-7-0

Printed in Korea